FLIP TO SIDE B AND BE BOLD AS A LION

A Simple, Surefire Way to Maximize Your Confidence with People

VAUGHN KOHLER

Printed in the United States of America

ISBN: 978-0-9978121-0-7

First Edition

14 13 12 11 10 / 10 9 8 7 6 5 4 3 2 1

INTRODUCTION
TO *POINTS OF IMPACT*
THE **BOOKLET SERIES**

I could quote experts and studies and statistics on the relevance of interpersonal skills to success and happiness, but isn't it common sense? All other factors being equal, the following is undeniably true:

- If you're good with people, you will be more successful at friendship and love.

- If you're good with people, you'll be more successful at work.

- If you're good with people, you'll make a positive impact on the world.

- If you make a positive impact on the world, you'll feel your life has meaning.

- If you feel your life has meaning, you'll be happy.

THE PURPOSE OF THE POINTS

Flip to Side B and Be Bold as A Lion is the first of six booklets in the *Points of Impact series*. Future topics include developing compelling character and conduct. The purpose of the entire series is to help you engage people more profoundly so that you can impact the world more powerfully.

The purpose of *Points of Impact* is to help you engage people more profoundly so that you can impact the world more powerfully.

Points of Impact helps advance my specific mission in life, which is "to help men and women maximize their impact for their gain and the good of the world."

FOR YOUR GAIN

When I say "for their gain," I'm serious. I want the principles and practices you learn in this booklet (and all my resources) *to personally and practically benefit you*—whether that means you:

- Attract more people
- Achieve greater influence in society
- Earn greater income
- Or whatever!

AND THE GOOD OF THE WORLD

But I don't want it to be one-sided. It's not all about you—and I think you know that. The other part of the equation is that your gain should result in the good of the world. Who would deny that our world could use some help?

VAUGHN KOHLER

**The other part of the equation is that your gain
should result in the good of the world.**

Maybe it is just me, but our world seems crazier and more dangerous than ever. We may not all agree on the root cause of the many problems facing us, but let's work together to discover some reasonable solutions. As G.K. Chesterton once wrote, "We men and women are all in the same boat, upon a stormy sea. We owe to each other a terrible and tragic loyalty."

PROFOUND AND PRACTICAL
I know full well that there are many resources out there to help you develop your interpersonal skills and improve your ability to influence and impact the world. But to be honest, I feel like they are either deep and complicated *or* shallow and sales-y. I want to create resources that are both profound and practical.

COMPELLING, NOT CLICHÉ
I also want them to be compelling, not cliché; so for this series, I've worked hard to draw from many different sources of insight—from epic Greek poetry and 80s music to the parables of Jesus and John Cusack movies.

I'M HERE TO HELP
Bottom line: if I can help you, I want to. This series is meant to impact you so that you can impact others. If what you're holding in your hand doesn't help you, I'll be

sad—but I'll get over it and try harder. If if does help you; if it benefits you and results in greater good for the world, then I'll be thrilled.

This series is meant to impact you so that you can impact others.

Feel free to contact me with your questions, comments, glowing feedback, or snide remarks. You can find me online at www.vaughnkohler.com. You can also learn more about me and my work in the back of this booklet.

Best regards,

Vaughn Kohler
St. Louis, Missouri
June 2016

"YOU CAN ENGAGE
ANYTIME, MAVERICK"

There are many different personality types. There are also many different ways that men and women approach and interact with other people. But, more often than not, even the most outgoing among us can find ourselves acting like Maverick after Goose died.

You know about Maverick, don't you? I'm referring to the lead character in the movie, *Top Gun*. Maverick, played by Tom Cruise, is a cocky naval fighter pilot whose confidence is shaken when his best friend and RIO (Radar Intercept Officer) Goose is killed in an air combat training accident. Shortly after the ordeal, Maverick is sent back up in the air to continue his fighter pilot duties. But he loses the edge. Time and time again, he goes up into the sky, flies around in circles, but doesn't fly headlong into the thick of combat. A critical scene in the movie unfolds like this:

[Jester is the flight instructor on the ground in communication through radio. Sundown is Maverick's new RIO/Co-pilot.]

Jester: Come on, kid. Come on. Get in there and engage.

Sundown: Okay, you've got a bogey at 2 o'clock low, Maverick. You got the angle. Piece of cake, pal.

Jester: Take the shot. Take the shot!

Sundown: You can engage any time, Maverick.

[Maverick is near catatonic and unresponsive. Then he veers away from the combat.]

Sundown: Hey, where the hell are you going?

Maverick: It's not good. No. It doesn't look good.

Sundown: What do you mean it doesn't look good? It doesn't get to look any better than that!

Maverick: No. It doesn't look good.

[Maverick lands and never engages the enemy.]

Eventually, Maverick gets his mojo back and in true 1980s Cold War style, he opens up a can of whoop-ass on a handful of Soviet fighters. All's well that ends well with Maverick and the United States of America.

But what about you?

To be successful in anything, we have to engage life. We have to fly in and go one-on-one with people, and we need to do it skillfully and with purpose. But we have to be willing to engage in the first place.

To be successful in anything, we have to engage life.

Do you always engage? Do you fly headlong into encounters and relationships with people who are going to help make you successful and happy?

If you are someone who wants to enjoy meaningful relationships, do you engage?

Or do you say, "No. No. It's not good. It doesn't look good."?

If you are someone who wants to achieve great goals in life, do you boldly contact and connect with people who can help you on the road to success?

Or do you say, "No. No. It's not good. It doesn't look good."?

If you are a salesperson who wants to increase your sales quota, do you overcome your fear and increase your bottom line?

Or do you say, "No. No. It's not good. It doesn't look good."?

If you are an entrepreneur or business person, do you realize that administrative skill and good business sense will not cut it? Do you understand that you must boldly engage the people in the marketplace and meaningfully connect with the public?

Or do you say, "No, no. It's not good. It doesn't look good."?

To be as happy and successful as we want to be, we have to have confidence—confidence to engage and connect with people. We have to be bold in talking to them; whether they are a potential customer, our boss, or the man or woman of our dreams. Yes. We need confidence! We need the strongest, most unshakeable confidence possible.

This little booklet is designed to provide you a simple, surefire way to maximize your confidence with people.

The truth is, I believe the conventional wisdom for building confidence is helpful, but it is insufficient. There's a whole different way—in some ways, a far more effective and reliable way—to increase your confidence. But I'm guessing if you are like most people, you aren't aware of it and aren't using it. That's too bad; because you are neglecting an incredibly powerful source for increasing your boldness with people.

Let me explain . . .

A RECORD
AND A REALIZATION

Like other elementary school boys in the 1980s, I loved *Rocky 3*. I laughed as Rocky Balboa (Sylvester Stallone) taunted the savage but stupid Clubber Lang (Mr. T, fool!) in the final round of the fight—I cheered as he cut him down right jab by left hook—and finally knocked him out.

While the movie was exciting, the theme song performed by *Survivor* was even better: "Eye of the Tiger"! For my birthday, my parents bought me the single, and I listened to it so much I almost wore out the vinyl 45. Over and over again, I blared the song from my cheap Emerson record player. Whether I was pretending to be a prize fighter, a knight of Minas Tirith, or one of the Super Friends, it pumped me up and readied me for combat. Every now and then, it motivated me in other, less violent ways, as when it inspired me to play harder on the Morgan Monster soccer team or talk to one of the prettier girls in Mrs. McNaul's 4th grade class.

Two years later, I was rummaging through my music collection, trying to figure out what to listen to, when it suddenly dawned on me: My *Rocky 3* record had two sides. I had always rocked out to "Eye of the Tiger," but I didn't even know what was on Side B. I flipped the record over, placed it on the turntable, and for the first time in my life listened to "Take You On a Saturday."

The song possessed Survivor's trademark qualities: hard-driving guitar, passionate vocals, and a high energy, harmonic refrain. But lyrically, it was far different. Instead of fighting and rivalry, it focused on feelings and romance. Instead of *hanging tough* and *staying hungry*, it spoke of *holding you close* and *lovin' til Monday*. The whole record was about passion. Side A was about competition. Side B was about love.

I discovered that both songs were incredible.

But I would never have experienced the second song if I hadn't remembered *to flip the record over.*

VAUGHN KOHLER

THE COMMON SIDE
OF CONFIDENCE

As we seek to build confidence in engaging others in conversation, most of us make an error similar to the one I made with my *Rocky 3* record. We mistakenly believe that the method is one-sided. The vast majority of motivational mavens and self-help gurus confirm this mistaken notion: What is supremely important, we are told, is what we believe about *ourselves:*

- I am special
- I have a unique experience
- I have a valuable perspective
- I am entitled to my opinions
- I have important thoughts to share
- I am fully capable of meaningful self-expression

When it comes to confidence, it's not that any of these individual statements is wrong as much as together they are insufficient. If you base your confidence entirely on your beliefs about yourself, your confidence will be one-sided, and thus imbalanced. It will be lop-sided, leaning too heavily inward. What happens when our focus is on ourselves? Two things: and neither is helpful in building confidence. The first is that our self-focus degenerates into self-consciousness. In looking at ourselves so intently and consistently, we don't just see our strengths. If we are honest with ourselves, we see our weaknesses, too: our inconsistencies, hypocrisies, and shortcomings.

We have such a close-up view of ourselves that our constant inward focus begins to make our inward qualities seem bigger than they really are. It's like the movie *Ant-Man*, when Scott Lang shrinks down to insect size for the first time, and the world around him becomes super-sized. Even small objects like sugar cubes appear enormous.

That's what happens when we focus only on ourselves. Everything seems gigantic. Our weaknesses seem gigantic; and we become overly sensitive. Our strengths seem gigantic; and we become arrogant. Over-sensitivity prevents us from approaching others, and our arrogance keeps others from wanting to approach us!

That's what happens when we focus only on ourselves. Everything seems gigantic.

Over-sensitivity prevents us from approaching others, and our arrogance keeps others from wanting to approach us!

VAUGHN KOHLER

GIVE BOTH SIDES ^{OF}CONFIDENCE EQUAL PLAYING TIME

The solution to this is to give both sides of your confidence equal playing time. We do this by realizing that there's another side to confidence—a Side B—and we commit ourselves to regularly "playing" that side. If Side A of confidence focuses on what we believe about ourselves, the focus of Side B is *what we believe about others*. Yes, right belief about others is a stand-up, surefire way to maximize our confidence.

How does what we believe about others affect our confidence? Consider this: most of us look at other people in three ways:

- Idols to be worshipped
- Addictions to be abused
- Tools to be used

THE THREE ENSLAVING BELIEFS ABOUT PEOPLE

These are what I call The Three Enslaving Beliefs About People. Let's look closer at each Enslaving Belief:

1. People are idols to be worshipped. Do you know what an idol is? If you're my age, you might think of the legendary Billy Idol of "White Wedding" *and* "Rebel Yell" fame. Nowadays, when most people hear the word "idol" they think of Simon Cowell and *American Idol*. Common sense tells us that the word "idol" is now associated with fame, popularity, and being the center of the universe. Well, idols in the general religious sense could simply be wooden or stone representations of deities, but in the sacred writings of the Jewish people, an idol was a *false god*. It wrongly served as the center of someone's universe. It didn't deserve to be there.

We often turn people into idols. Practically speaking, they become the center of our universe. Our happiness becomes contingent on them. When this happens, we form a certain master/slave relationship with them. That's because so much of who we are is invested in them. Since we "worship" them as a god or goddess, our mood and our actions are bound to their mood and actions toward us. If they are happy with us, we're confident. If they express detachment or disdain toward us, our confidence plummets. The problem is that we are too invested in them to develop and maintain our own sense of self. We want to make them happy *no matter what*. We want their approval *at all costs*. With so many variables in play at any given time, maintaining peak levels of confidence is well near impossible.

Since we "worship" them as a god or goddess, our mood and our actions are bound to their mood and actions toward us.

VAUGHN KOHLER

2. People are addictions to be abused. This is similar to viewing others as idols, but with a slight difference. Whereas we want to please our idols, we need to *possess* our addictions. Anybody who has ever had experience with, or known somebody with, an addiction—whether it is to alcohol, pornography, gambling, or otherwise—knows that person is enslaved to their need for it. Of course, everybody needs other people. Where the need becomes problematic is when it rises above normal interpersonal levels. This is what experts call *codependency*. I just call it being an especially needy person who has an unhealthy attachment to another person. You see this a lot with insecure guys who let pretty girls completely take advantage of them—simply because that guy believes he "needs" a beautiful woman in his life, to validate him as a person. Once again, what is created by this need is a kind of bondage, an enslavement to another.

This is a worst case scenario, but consider the analogy of the creature Gollum from *Lord of the Rings*. When he possessed his "Precious," the One Ring, he was happy (as happy as an addict can be), but when he didn't possess it, he was miserable. Ultimately, his need to possess the Ring led to his destruction.

To whatever extent you believe that another person is absolutely critical to your happiness, your happiness will always be contingent on them.

Hopefully, you won't ever feel toward anyone what Gollum felt toward his "Precious." But to whatever extent you believe that another person is absolutely critical to your happiness, your happiness will always be contingent on them. And if your happiness is contingent on them, you will never experience peak levels of confidence in your relationship with them.

3. People are tools to be used. The third Enslaving Belief about other people is that they are tools to be used. Of course, most decent human beings don't overtly regard others like this, but it is a temptation from time to time to believe that other people are simply means to whatever ends we seek. We have things we want to do, goals we want to accomplish, dreams that we want fulfilled—and we regard certain individuals as our ticket to the big show, our gravy train, our way of getting what we want. Since we believe this about them, we justify deception and manipulation.

But here's why that doesn't work: deep down in our hearts, unless we are sociopaths, we know that it's wrong to use other people. And our conscience is chained up with the realization that we are acting like a bad person and doing a wrong thing. Here's the deal: an uneasy conscience undermines confidence. When we know we are in the wrong, it's hard to be bold in the way we live. Of course, we can willfully choose to do something wrong, even though we know it's wrong; but in the end, that affects us. And we will inevitably become the kind of people we don't want to be—and we won't attract others to us.

Deep down in our hearts, unless we are sociopaths,
we know that it's wrong to use other people.
An uneasy conscience undermines confidence.

Unlike the other two Enslaving Beliefs, we don't bind ourselves to other people—we bind ourselves to *our own uneasy conscience*. We burden our own sense of right and wrong, and we can no more engage people with full confidence than we could run swiftly and easily through a bog of quicksand.

For good evidence supporting the fact that everyone has a basic sense of right and wrong, check out the appendix of *The Abolition of Man* by C.S. Lewis, where he lists the codes of conduct held by all cultures throughout the centuries. Lewis was a committed Christian, but people in every field agree—from anthropologists like Donald Brown to cognitive neuroscientists like Joshua Greene—that a sense of right and wrong is hard-wired into the human race. *Who, what,* or *how* it is hard-wired may be up for discussion and debate. But the fact remains: the sense of right and wrong is *there*.

As you can see, these three common, yet Enslaving Beliefs About People undermine confidence. They place us in bondage to other people—and to the darker aspects of ourselves. There is, however, a belief we can have about other people that liberates us to be confident in every encounter we have with another human being. It is the liberating belief that human beings *are gifts to us*; and those gifts are meant to be valued and enjoyed.

There is a belief we can have about other people that liberates us to be confident in every encounter ... the liberating belief that human beings *are gifts to us*.

NECESSARY VS. PURE GIFTS

Before I go into an explanation of how regarding other people as gifts help us maximize our confidence, I want to make an important distinction between what I'll call *necessary* gifts and *pure* gifts. An example of a necessary gift is a hamburger that you give a homeless person who is starving. That's a gift, insofar as the homeless person did not pay for it and you did not hand it over to him under compulsion. It was extended to him freely. Nevertheless, there is still a sense in which the gift was necessary; otherwise, if no one ever gave this starving homeless man a hamburger, he would eventually die.

Pure gifts, on the other hand, are things that are extended completely of our own free will and are not necessary to our basic survival. So, pretty much anything beyond food, shelter, and clothing is a pure gift. If you gave someone a ring, it's a gift. So is a bike, a train set, an exercise ball, and a pair of movie tickets. You get the point. (Actually, many of the things we consider necessary gifts are not necessary at all. I'm sure there are a lot of people who think a car and a cell phone are necessities in today's modern world. But technically, they aren't. You could do without them and still survive. Having or not having them will determine the quality of your life; but it doesn't determine whether or not you will live.)

Now, I know that when we come to the issue of human beings, immediately someone with good insight will say, "Well, I can see how other people could be regarded as both necessary gifts and pure gifts." You are right. We are by our nature interpersonal, social creatures, and human interaction is necessary to our health. Isolation and loneliness has serious physical and psychological consequences. In fact, when we are babies, we can actually die from lack of human touch. That's how essential other people are to our well-being!

On the other hand, let me ask you this about your most satisfying relationships in life: aren't they based on simple enjoyment and not dire need? Common sense tells us that two people who are forced to be in a room together and coerced into getting along are not going to have a positive experience. On the other hand, when two people freely agree to get together, with no strings attached, and mutually agree to enjoy one another's company, isn't this how our most satisfying, happiness-inspiring relationships operate? Yes, it is. And we have a word for these kinds of relationships: friendships. C.S. Lewis said, "Friendship is unnecessary, like philosophy, like art. It has no survival value; rather, it is one of those things that gives value to survival." This is exactly why we very often refer to our best friendships as "gifts."

C.S. Lewis said,
"Friendship is unnecessary, like philosophy, like art.
It has no survival value; rather, it is one of those things
that gives value to survival."

This is exactly why we very often refer to our best friendships as "gifts."

Also, consider this: the strongest marriages are built on friendship. Suppose a couple is sitting together and the husband wants to be physically intimate with his wife. Which approach is going to work better?

Husband: I have biological needs that need to be satisfied. Can we have sex?

Or

Husband: You are so beautiful. I love how you make me feel. Would you enjoy making love tonight as much as I would?

Obviously, the moment things become compulsive, they are ruined. But relationships are the happiest and most satisfying when people freely give of themselves.

THE FRIENDSHIP PRINCIPLE

Here is the key:

The principle that is at work in friendship (and love) should be harnessed and used to maximize your confidence with people.

Friendship is a relationship where two people freely give of themselves to one another. It is a relationship based on freedom; and if you are guided by that same basic principle of freedom in all your relationships, you will have the confidence to approach, engage, and meaningfully connect with any person, no matter who they are and what position they hold in your life.

HOW BELIEVING PEOPLE ARE GIFTS HELPS YOU

At this point, you may be wondering how believing that people are gifts helps you maximize your confidence with them. Here's how:

1. You possess a healthy detachment. Remember the classic comedy, *Tommy Boy*? The immortal Chris Farley plays Tommy Callahan, a happy but hapless recent college grad who is learning the ropes of sales, and trying to take over his father's business. In the early stages, things go badly—really badly—with his sales calls. He is tied up in knots, he's so nervous, so he crashes and burns again and again and again.

But then Tommy and his colleague Richard Hayden (played by David Spade) pull off the highway to eat at a diner. As they eat, they lament their failure; and Tommy decides he really wants chicken wings. He tries to order some from the waitress, who is cold and curt.

Tommy: I'll have chicken wings.

Waitress: Kitchen's closed until dinner. I just got cold stuff and desserts.

Tommy: Boy, some chicken wings would really hit the spot. You sure it's closed?

Waitress: Let me check. *[Does nothing.]* Yup, it's closed.

Tommy: Okay. I'll just have a sugar packet or two. Hey, what's your name?

Waitress: Helen.

Tommy: That's nice. You look like a Helen. Helen, we're both in sales. Let me tell you why I suck as a salesman.

[Tommy then goes on a hilarious, self-deprecating rant expressing his frustration at his total lack of success in sales. When he is done, Helen's whole demeanor has changed from bad to good.]

Waitress: Tell you what, I'll go turn the fryers back on and throw some wings in for ya.

Tommy: Thanks, Helen! Tommy like-y. Tommy want wing-y.

[Richard is amazed. He can't believe the powerful effect Tommy had on the waitress.]

Richard: That turnaround you just pulled off with that waitress! Why can't you sell like that?

[Tommy shrugs his shoulders.]

Tommy: I'm just having fun. If we didn't get the wings, so what? We still got that meat-lovers' pizza in the trunk.

[Richard shakes his head.]

Richard: No, you got the wings because you're relaxed. You had confidence.

There is huge wisdom in the dialogue between Tommy and Richard. In fact, the lesson of the scene is priceless. Tommy is detached and that makes him effective. And that's the lesson for us. To put it frankly, we are the most confident when we don't care! Ancient masters of rhetoric (the art of persuasion) used to call this the "posture of indifference," and it is profoundly effective.

**We are the most confident when we don't care!
Ancient masters of rhetoric (the art of persuasion) used to call this
the "posture of indifference," and it is profoundly effective.**

When you regard other people as pure gifts, that drives detachment. It means that you place no external conditions on your happiness. You are not weighed down by the burden of an agenda. You are completely free. And here's the key: you are not free because you are so confident in what you believe about yourself. *You are free because of what you believe about the other person!*

2. You are free from an uneasy conscience. Wasn't it Bob Marley who said, "Emancipate yourself from mental slavery" or something like that? The truth is, I have no idea what he meant exactly. The only think I know about Bob Marley is that he smoked dope and wore dreadlocks. But I do like the phrase "mental slavery." As I wrote earlier, one real form of mental slavery that affects our confidence is an uneasy conscience. We can be physically, mentally, and emotionally weighed down by our consciences. That's a scientific fact. According to psychologists, signs of suppressed guilt include distraction, loss of energy, tarnished self-image, and depleted joy. These, in turn, make us more self-conscious and overly sensitive.

How do you think all this affects your confidence? A lot. Unless you're Josef Mengele, Hannibal Lecter, or Charles Manson, each of us has a pretty decent conscience. If you're a normal person, you can't treat people like idols, addictions, or tools, because deep down you'll know that *it is wrong to do so*. You can try to suppress your conscience, but it will still be there, weighing you down like an anchor and sinking your attempts to relate to people.

On the other hand, when you regard people as gifts; when you seek to enjoy them for who they are, with no strings attached, and truly place value on them, *you are freed*. There is a paradox here: you are confident when you don't care. But when you truly care about people, you become care-free. *You are liberated!* And that freedom of conscience translates into profound confidence to engage and connect with others, no matter who they are. An ancient Middle Eastern proverb put it this way: "Those who live right are bold as a lion!"

There is a paradox here:
you are confident when you don't care.
But when you truly care about people, you become care-free.

VAUGHN KOHLER

LIBERATED
TO BE A LION

So we come to this: if you believe the right things about yourself, you'll have self-confidence—the "Eye of the Tiger" kind of confidence. That's important, but insufficient. But if you "flip to Side B" and build your confidence on what you believe about others—that they are gifts meant to be valued and enjoyed—then you will bring your confidence into balance. It will be fully maximized. You won't just have the "Eye of the Tiger." Now your confidence will be rock steady and unflinching.

You'll be bold as a lion.

AN IMPORTANT POSTSCRIPT

What I've shared with you can't just be affirmed intellectually. We have to actually believe it in our heart of hearts. As they say, "repetition is the mother of learning." In addition to repeating the words below—as a kind of pledge or mantra, if you will—reflect on them until they fully shape how you think and act.

People are not idols to be worshipped.
I will treat no human person as the god of my life.

People are not addictions to be abused.
I will have no unhealthy attachment to anyone.

People are not tools to be used.
I will not use others for my own selfish gain.

The men and women I encounter today are gifts in my life.
I will value them. I will enjoy them.

Free of conditions, hidden agendas, and an uneasy conscience,
I will engage everyone with full confidence and joy.

ABOUT THE AUTHOR

Vaughn Kohler is a professional writer, ghost writer, speaker, and communications consultant who considers himself "the point man for people of impact." Whether his clients are c-level executives or spiritual leaders, his mission is "to help men and women maximize their impact for their gain and the good of the world." He has been a pastor, magazine editor, marketing specialist, development director, and college-level Communications instructor. He holds degrees in communications, religion, and creative writing. He lives in St. Louis, Missouri. Find him online at vaughnkohler.com.

Connect with him:

Facebook   www.facebook.com/vaughn.kohler

Twitter   @vaughnkohler

Instagram   @vaughnkohler

BOOK VAUGHN KOHLER
TO SPEAK **YOUR EVENT**
AT

Vaughn has delivered hundreds of messages and presentations to nonprofit organizations, college students, church groups, and businesses.

He makes things thought-provoking but easy-to-understand; he tells stories, asks questions, uses memorable analogies, and draws wisdom and insights from diverse sources, from Jesus of Nazareth to Steve Jobs.

He wants to equip and inspire his audiences to achieve greater success and happiness; to maximize their impact for their gain and the good of the world.

SPEAKING TOPICS
Vaughn will help you…

- Maximize your confidence to fully engage those around you
- Build rapport with others to build a better career, business, and life
- Infuse every interpersonal encounter with magic and meaning
- Transform the world through compelling acts of kindness

SPEECHES, SEMINARS, ETC.

To get on Vaughn's schedule, send an email to:
Vaughn@vaughnkohler.com

www.vaughnkohler.com